MY NEW PET

MY PET CAT

BY NANCY GREENWOOD

Gareth Stevens
PUBLISHING

Please visit our website, www.garethstevens.com. For a free color catalog of all our high-quality books, call toll free 1-800-542-2595 or fax 1-877-542-2596.

Portions of this work were originally authored by Cecelia H. Brannon and published as Pet Cats. All new material this edition authored by Nancy Greenwood.

Library of Congress Cataloging-in-Publication Data
Names: Greenwood, Nancy, author.
Title: My pet cat / Nancy Greenwood.
Description: New York : Gareth Stevens Publishing, [2023] | Series: My new pet | Includes index.
Identifiers: LCCN 2021061242 | ISBN 9781538280928 (set) | ISBN 9781538280935 (library binding) | ISBN 9781538280911 (paperback) | ISBN 9781538280942 (ebook)
Subjects: LCSH: Cats–Juvenile literature.
Classification: LCC SF445.7 .G74 2023 | DDC 636.8–dc23/eng/20220111
LC record available at https://lccn.loc.gov/2021061242

Published in 2023 by
Gareth Stevens Publishing
29 East 21st Street
New York, NY 10010

Designer: Andrea Davison-Bartolotta
Editor: Kristen Nelson

Photo credits: Cover, p.1 lenajaron/Shutterstock.com; series art (interior backgrounds) Magnia/Shutterstock.com; p. 5 threewhitecats/Shutterstock.com; p. 7 (top) Peterpancake/Shutterstock.com; p. 7 (bottom left) Xseon/Shutterstock.com; p. 7 (bottom right) Nils Jacobi/Shutterstock.com; p. 9 Anna Andersson Fotografi/Shutterstock.com; p. 11 Alexander Sobol/Shutterstock.com; p. 13 Olga Smolina SL/Shutterstock.com; p. 15 Brenda Carson/Shutterstock.com; p. 17 Jason Kolenda/Shutterstock.com; p. 19 Alena Ozerova/
Shutterstock.com; p. 21 Dimaris/Shutterstock.com.

Printed in the United States of America

CONTENTS

Boldface words appear in the glossary.

Your Pet Cat

Having a pet is a big **responsibility**. You need to be able to care for it. This means feeding it and making sure it has enough water. It also means keeping it clean and healthy. Cats can be great pets!

Cats can have fur in many colors. They can be black, white, gray, brown, orange, or a mix of these colors. Some cats do not have any fur at all! Cats often make a sound called a purr. This means they are happy.

Kitten Around

Cats are very small when they are born. Baby cats are called kittens. **Newborn** kittens get food from their mother's milk. If the mother is not around, you can feed a kitten special food in place of their mother's milk.

Playtime!

Many kittens like to play with toys. Adult cats like to play too! Cats often like toys they can chase. Toys on strings can be fun for cats. Cats love a plant called **catnip**. Many cat toys have catnip inside of them.

Bath Time!

Most cats don't like getting wet or going in water. Luckily, they don't need to take baths. They keep themselves clean by licking their fur. Pet cats use a special box as their bathroom. It is called a litter box.

Feeding Your Cat

You'll need to feed your cat every day. They like meat and fish. Sometimes their food is dry **kibble**. Sometimes it is wet and comes in a can. A **veterinarian** can help you find the best food for your cat.

Free Time for Cats

Cats have claws that help them climb. They like to **scratch** things with their claws too. You can get special posts or toys for your cat to scratch. Scratching is good for cats and helps keep them healthy.

For many cats, a favorite thing to do is sleep. Some of them sleep for 16 hours a day! If your cat starts sleeping more than normal, you may want to have the veterinarian check on your cat.

Staying Healthy

Pets need to go to the doctor just like you. All pet cats should go to the veterinarian once a year for a **checkup**. If your cat ever seems sick, the veterinarian can help then too. A healthy cat is a happy cat!

GLOSSARY

catnip: A type of mint that has a strong smell and is attractive to cats.

checkup: A visit to the doctor to see if a person or animal is healthy.

kibble: Ground meal or grain often shaped into pellets and used for animal food.

newborn: Recently born.

responsibility: Something a person is in charge of.

scratch: To rub a surface or object with something sharp, such as one's nails or claws.

veterinarian: A doctor who is trained to treat animals.

FOR MORE INFORMATION

BOOKS

Emminizer, Theresa. *Is a Cat a Good Pet for Me?* New York, NY: PowerKids Press, 2020.

Geister-Jones, Sophie. *Cats*. Minneapolis, MN: Cody Koala, 2020.

Salzmann, Mary Elizabeth. *Cats Are Fun!* Minneapolis, MN: Abdo Publishing, 2021.

WEBSITES

Cats
www.ducksters.com/animals/cats.php
Go to this website to learn more about cats.

Domestic Cats
www.dkfindout.com/us/animals-and-nature/cats/domestic-cats/
Find out more about domestic, or pet, cats on this website.

INDEX